He Is Alive!

A Picture Book on the Last Week of Jesus' Life & His Resurrection

Written by

Helen Haidle

Illustrated by

Joel Spector

Zonder**kidz**

The Children's Group of Zondervan Publishing House

To Alison and Rachael
It's a blessing to know you. Your lives truly show
that you believe Jesus IS alive!
–H.H.

To John and Rena Adsit
Whose love and faith have enriched my life
–J.S.

He Is Alive!
Copyright 2001 by Helen Haidle
Illustrations, copyright 2001 by Joel Spector
Requests for information should be addressed to:

Zonderkidz ™
The Children's Group of Zondervan Publishing House

Grand Rapids, MI 49530
www.zonderkidz.com

ISBN 0-310-70033-7

All Scripture quotations, unless otherwise indicated, are taken from the HOLY BIBLE,
NEW INTERNATIONAL READER'S VERSION ® Copyright © 1994, 1996 by International Bible Society.
Used by permission of Zondervan Publishing House. All rights reserved.

Editor: Gwen Ellis
Art Direction and Design: Lisa Workman

Printed in China
00 01 02 03 04 / 1 2 3 4 5

Introduction

God sent his Son, Jesus, to the earth. Do you know why?

Jesus came to bring us God's love and forgiveness. He lived a perfect and obedient life. He helped people, taught them about God, healed the sick, and performed miracles. What he did here on earth was important. But what he did at the end of his life was even more important.

Jesus took one last trip to Jerusalem to finish his work on earth. Come along, let's follow him during the last week of his life. Then you will know how much he loves you.

He lived ... he died ... and he came alive again—all for YOU!

A Plot Begins

Mary and Martha sent word to Jesus. Their brother Lazarus was very, very sick. They knew he was dying and only Jesus could save him.

But Jesus waited to come. When he finally arrived, Lazarus was dead. Jesus went to the tomb where many people were weeping. He wept, too. Then he said loudly, "Move the stone away!"

The men groaned and strained as they pushed back the stone.

"Lazarus, come out!" Jesus shouted into the open grave.

Something stirred way back in the tomb. A sound! Could it be the shuffling of feet? Yes! Lazarus, wrapped in burial cloth, hobbled out.

"Unwrap him," said Jesus. Everyone cheered and ran to help.

Right then the Jewish priests and teachers began to plot against Jesus. "More people follow him every day," they grumbled. "We must find a way to kill him…and Lazarus, too."

Who Is He?

A few days after Jesus raised Lazarus, he said to his disciples, "Let's go up to Jerusalem and celebrate."

Hundreds of people were also on their way to take part in the Passover Feast. When they found out that Jesus was coming, they cut branches off the palm trees and ran to meet him.

Waving branches, they shouted, "Praise to the Son of David! Blessed is the one who comes in the name of the Lord!"

They spread their coats on the road like a carpet to honor him as king.

"Hosanna!" they cried. "Blessed is the King of Israel!" The noise was deafening as Jesus entered the gate of Jerusalem. It stirred up the whole city.

Those jealous priests and teachers watched the scene and went on planning how they could get rid of Jesus. "Look!" they said, "the whole world is following him."

Trouble in the Temple!

On Monday morning, Jesus walked into the courtyard around the temple. The courtyard was filled with birds and sheep being sold for offerings. There were also money changers taking money from those who came from far away places and changing it into the money of the land.

When Jesus saw what was going on, he grabbed the corner of a money changer's table and flipped it over! Coins clattered and clanged as they hit the ground and rolled across the courtyard stones.

"What do you think you're doing?" shouted the money changers.

Jesus turned over more tables and benches. Crash! Bang! Clatter! Cages broke open and the doves flew away. Birds squawked and sheep baahed.

Jesus chased the money changers out of the temple. He shouted after them, "The Lord says that his house is to be a place of prayer. But you robbers have cheated his people!"

It was a day the money changers would never forget! Neither would the priests and teachers. They couldn't wait to get rid of Jesus.

The Betrayer Comes

Every day Jesus went back to the temple and taught all those who would listen about the kingdom of God. The priests and leaders also listened to everything Jesus said.

One day Jesus pointed right at them and shouted, "You are blind fools! You hypocrites and pretenders! You look so good on the outside. But inside, you are greedy and rotten! How will you escape God's punishment?"

Oh, did the priests and leaders get angry! They wanted to arrest Jesus as soon as possible. "We must take him away," they decided, "so the crowds won't start a fight."

At that time, Judas, a disciple of Jesus, came to them. "I can help you find Jesus when he is alone," Judas offered. "What will you pay me?"

The chief priests counted out thirty silver coins for Judas. From then on he looked for the right time and place to betray Jesus.

Washing Dusty Feet

On Thursday, Peter and John prepared a meal of roasted lamb and bread for the Passover Feast. Jesus and the disciples joined them in the Upper Room. Before they ate, Jesus took a bowl of water and began to wash his disciples' feet. This was usually a servant's job. Afterwards, he explained, "I have given you an example of serving. Now serve each other as I have served you."

At the end of the meal, Jesus took some bread. He gave thanks to God, broke it, and gave it to his disciples. "This is my body," he said. "It is given for you. Every time you eat it, remember me."

Then he lifted up a cup, gave thanks, and handed it to them. "This is my blood of the new promise," he said. "It is poured out to forgive the sins of many people. When you drink it, remember me."

After singing a hymn of thanks, they went up to the Garden of Gethsemane.

In the Garden

As they walked, Jesus warned them, "Tonight you will all leave me."

"Not I!" Peter protested. "All the others may leave. But I never will!"

Jesus said, "Before the rooster crows, you will deny me three times."

"No!" Peter said. "I am ready to die with you. I'll never deny you!"

When they entered the Garden, Jesus said, "Sit here while I go and pray."

Going a little farther, he fell with his face to the ground and prayed in great sorrow, "My Father, if it is possible, take this terrible suffering away from me. But let what you want be done, not what I want."

Twice Jesus returned and found his disciples sleeping. Each time he went away and prayed again. The third time he prayed, an angel from heaven came and strengthened him. Now Jesus prayed even harder. He knew what was going to happen. His sweat fell to the ground as great drops of blood.

When he returned, he woke his disciples. "Get up," he said. "Here come my betrayer and my enemies."

An Unfair Trial

A large crowd carrying clubs, swords, and torches entered the Garden. Judas came over to Jesus and kissed him on the cheek. Judas did this to show the soldiers who Jesus was. When the soldiers tried to arrest Jesus, Peter jerked out his sword and cut off a man's ear.

"Put away your sword!" commanded Jesus as he healed the ear. "Peter, don't you know I can ask my heavenly Father for help? He could send an army of angels."

Then Jesus let the soldiers tie his hands. And all the disciples, even Peter, ran away.

The soldiers took Jesus to the house of Caiaphas, the high priest, where angry teachers accused Jesus falsely. They told many lies about him.

Finally Caiaphas asked Jesus, "What do you have to say for yourself?"

When Jesus said nothing, Caiaphas demanded, "By the living God, I command you to tell us the truth. Are you the Messiah, the Son of God?"

Jesus spoke the truth. "I AM," he said.

Caiaphas shouted to the council, "You heard him! What's your verdict?"

"Guilty!" they shouted. "He must die!" Then they blindfolded Jesus and slapped him, saying, "If you're the Messiah, tell us who hit you!"

I Don't Know Him!

Peter followed far behind as they led Jesus to the high priest's house. While Jesus was on trial, Peter sat down by a fire in the courtyard.

A woman servant, who was standing near the fire, watched Peter closely. Finally she said, "This man was with Jesus!"

Peter strongly denied it. "Woman, I don't know him!"

A little later another servant said, "You are also one of Jesus' disciples!"

Peter's face reddened. "No!" he insisted. "I swear I am not!"

Then a third man said, "You have an accent. You must be one of them."

"I never knew the man!" Peter shouted. "I swear I am telling the truth."

While he was speaking, a rooster crowed. And Peter remembered what Jesus said: "Before the rooster crows, you will deny me three times."

Filled with sorrow, Peter rushed from the courtyard, weeping bitterly.

Crucify Him!

The sun was rising when the chief priests took Jesus to Pontius Pilate, the Roman governor. They angrily accused Jesus, saying, "This man is a criminal! He claims to be a king. He deserves to die!"

Jesus didn't say one word to defend himself.

Amazed at Jesus' silence, Pilate asked him, "Aren't you going to answer them? They've charged you with many crimes."

But Jesus still said nothing.

Pilate knew Jesus was innocent. He went out to the crowd that had gathered and said, "I always free one prisoner at Passover. Shall I release your 'King'?"

Now the priests and teachers of the law had persuaded the people to ask Pilate to set free a murderer named Barabbas. So the crowd shouted, "No! Release Barabbas!"

"But what should I do with Jesus?" asked Pilate. "I find him not guilty."

"Crucify him!" shouted the crowd. "Crucify him!"

So Pilate set Barabbas free. He sent Jesus with the soldiers to be whipped.

Mocking the King

The soldiers treated Jesus roughly as they led him to their headquarters. After tying his hands to a whipping pole, they whipped his back.

Because Pilate had called Jesus the "King of the Jews," the soldiers dressed him in a purple robe. They also cut off some thorny branches, twisted them into the shape of a crown, and shoved it on his head.

One soldier put a stick in his hand and mocked him, saying, "Here's your scepter, O king!" Others joined in, saying, "Hail, King of the Jews!"

They spit on Jesus and fell on their knees, pretending to honor him. Grabbing the stick out of his hand, they beat him on the head with it.

Once more, Pilate brought Jesus out to the crowd. He was wearing the crown of thorns and the purple robe. "Here he is," said Pilate.

"Away with him! Crucify him!" screamed the angry crowd. Pilate feared they would start a fight, so he handed Jesus over to be crucified.

Nailed to the Cross

Jesus and two other prisoners were each forced to carry the heavy wooden crossbeam for their own cross to a hill outside the city.

Because Jesus was so weak from being whipped, the soldiers forced a man named Simon to carry it.

It was nine o'clock in the morning when the sound of hammers echoed across the hills. Soldiers nailed Jesus' hands and feet to the cross. They nailed a sign above his head. It read: This is Jesus of Nazareth, King of the Jews.

The soldiers divided up Jesus' clothes. Since his robe was woven in one piece, they said, "Don't tear it. Let's gamble to see who gets it."

Instead of cursing the soldiers, Jesus prayed, "Father, forgive them. They don't know what they are doing."

The priests and teachers stood near the cross and made fun of Jesus. "He saved others but he can't save himself! Let him come down from the cross. Then we'll believe in him!"

Jesus Dies

"Save yourself!" cried one of the criminals. "And save us, too!"

But the other criminal scolded him. "We're getting what we deserve. But this man hasn't done anything wrong." Then he said to Jesus, "Remember me when you come into your kingdom."

Jesus promised him, "Today you'll be with me in paradise."

At noon, the whole earth was covered with darkness. Jesus called out in a loud voice, "My God, my God, why have you left me all alone?"

Later, at three o'clock, Jesus cried out, "It is finished!" He had done what he came to do.

Then Jesus bowed his head and said, "Father, I give my spirit into your hands." And he breathed his final breath.

Suddenly the earth trembled and shook. Rocks split apart. And at that very moment, the thick curtain in the temple ripped from top to bottom.

Filled with amazement, the Roman officer in charge of Jesus' crucifixion exclaimed, "This man was truly the Son of God!"

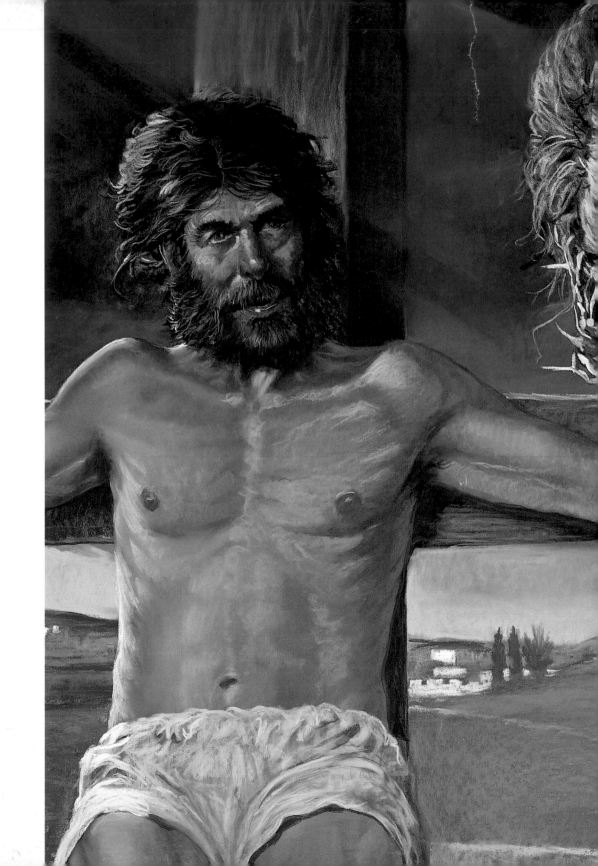

At the Tomb

The sun shone again as the crowd left. Only a few friends and some women who followed Jesus stayed to watch what would happen next.

A rich man named Joseph boldly asked Pilate for permission to bury the body of Jesus. Joseph brought some linen cloth and another man named Nicodemus brought seventy-five pounds of spices for the burial. They took Jesus' body down from the cross and carried it to a tomb in a nearby garden. Joseph had just finished carving this tomb for himself and his family.

The two men washed the body of Jesus and wrapped it in a long linen cloth. The spices and a sticky burial ointment were smeared on the cloth strips they wrapped around the body. They wrapped a smaller cloth around Jesus' head.

When the men finished, they rolled a huge stone over the door of the tomb. Meanwhile, some women stood nearby and watched.

Saturday Guard Duty

On Saturday the priests and teachers went to Pontius Pilate and said, "We remember a lie Jesus told. He promised, 'After three days I will rise again.' So you must order a guard for his tomb. If you don't, his disciples might steal the body and pretend that he is alive."

"Take some guards," Pilate said. "Make the tomb as secure as you can."

Before the Roman soldiers took up their guard duty, they opened the tomb to make sure Jesus' body was inside. Then, they rolled the stone back in place.

The guards stretched a cord across the large stone. Both ends of the cord were fastened with clay. They stamped the clay with the royal seal of Rome.

Now the priests were satisfied. No one would steal the body of Jesus.

No one dared to break the Roman seal—the punishment for doing so was instant death!

Surprise!

Very early on Sunday morning, a powerful earthquake struck the hill where Jesus was buried. The earth shuddered and trembled beneath the guards' feet. They shook with fear as a brilliant light flashed before them. They felt terrified!

An angel of the Lord came down from heaven. The angel's face and body shone like lightning. Its clothing gleamed bright as snow.

The guards took one look at the angel and collapsed in a heap, like dead men.

The angel broke the seal on the huge stone, hurled it away from the grave, and then sat down on top of the stone.

One look inside the grave showed that the body of Jesus was already gone! The grave clothes were empty.

He is alive!

Resurrection Morning

It was just after sunrise on Sunday morning when Mary Magdalene, along with Joanna, Salome, and several other women, came to the tomb bringing burial spices to put on Jesus' body.

As they walked to the grave, they asked each other, "Who will roll the stone away so we can go inside and anoint the body of Jesus?" (They didn't know that soldiers were guarding the tomb.) But when the women came near the grave, they saw the stone already rolled away!

Bravely, they ventured inside the tomb. The grave clothes lay there, but the wrappings were empty. The body of Jesus was missing!

Suddenly, two brightly shining angels appeared beside them.

"Don't be afraid," said an angel. "I know you are looking for Jesus who was crucified. He is not here! He has risen! Come and see the place where he was lying. Then go quickly and tell his disciples!"

He is alive!

Is It Really True?

The excited women headed back to the city of Jerusalem. Suddenly Jesus met them on the road and greeted them! They fell at his feet and worshiped him.

"Don't be afraid," Jesus said. "Go and tell my disciples."

The women were overjoyed! They ran to the disciples and told them everything. But the disciples just couldn't believe what the women said.

Peter and John wanted to see for themselves, so they raced to the tomb. When Peter rushed into the burial chamber, he saw a strange sight. The grave clothes were still neatly wrapped and undisturbed. The smaller cloth from around Jesus' head had been folded and placed by itself on the stone. Where was the body of Jesus?

Then John stepped inside and saw the grave clothes. He immediately believed! But he couldn't help wondering what had happened!

He is alive!

Surprising Appearances

Later that resurrection day, Jesus appeared to two followers. They didn't recognize him as he walked with them and talked with them. But when Jesus sat down to eat, he blessed the bread, and all at once they recognized him!

Then immediately he disappeared from their sight—and they knew: *He is alive!*

The two followers hurried to the Upper Room where the disciples huddled behind locked doors. As they started to tell how Jesus had appeared to them, Jesus suddenly stood among them and said, "Peace be with you."

The disciples were shocked and filled with fear. Was he a ghost?

"Why are you afraid?" asked Jesus. "Look at my hands and my feet. Touch me and see. A ghost doesn't have a body or bones like I do."

The men watched as Jesus ate some cooked fish. Then he talked with them and helped them understand why he had to suffer and die. And now they knew for sure: *He is alive!*

Will You Doubt ... or Believe?

Thomas, one of the disciples, was not there when Jesus appeared on Sunday night. He wouldn't believe the other disciples had seen Jesus.

"First I must see the nail marks in his hands," Thomas said. "I have to touch where the nails were. Only then will I believe what you say."

One week later, the disciples met together again. This time Thomas was with them. Suddenly Jesus came into the room, even though all the doors were locked.

He said to Thomas, "See my hands. Put your finger here where the nails were. Touch my wounds. Stop doubting—and believe!"

Thomas fell to his knees and cried out, "My Lord and my God!" Thomas didn't touch Jesus. He didn't have to. He knew Jesus was alive!

Jesus said to him, "Because you have seen me, you have believed. Blessed are those who have not seen me but still have believed."

He is alive!

JESUS IS ALIVE!

Jesus promised, "Because I live, you will live also."
John 14:19

Rejoice and be glad!
He IS alive!